Homophobia
<u>Deal with it</u>
and turn prejudice into pride

Steven Solomon • Illustrated by Nick Johnson

James Lorimer & Company Ltd., Publishers
Toronto

You're at school. The guy at the next locker is yelling at one of the kids trying to start up a Gay/Straight Alliance. "Get away from me, you fag. And stop looking at my body, if you don't want to get punched out!"

Your best friend is complaining about her soccer coach. "She works us too hard and loves to see us sweat. She must be a lesbo."

What do these things have in common? They are both examples of homophobia.

Homosexuality is when people are attracted to other people of the same sex in a physical or romantic way. It's when girls want to hook up with other girls, or when boys want to hook up with other boys. And you know that some people laugh at, tease, avoid, exclude, threaten or even target others who are gay or who they think are gay.

People who discriminate against, bully, harass or have it in for homosexuals are homophobic.

Whether you are gay or straight, you can be affected by homophobia. And this book can help you identify and deal with people who are homophobic.

Contents

What is Homopho

When you think of homophobia, do you think of gay bashing? Speaking out against allowing same-sex couples to get married or raise children? These are just two examples. Homophobia can be shown in a lot of other ways too. Homophobic people might . . .

- dislike someone just because that person is gay or lesbian
- use putdowns like "faggot," "queer" or "lesbo"
- avoid or say mean things about people with same-sex parents
- be afraid that gay kids of the same gender are going to come on to them
- target gay people
- think that lesbians and gays are failures as people
- believe that gay people don't deserve the same rights as everyone else
- make assumptions about sexual orientation based on what a person wears or how a person acts
- believe they are better than lesbian and gay people

bia?

Sometimes things that look homophobic are not necessarily examples of homophobia, like . . .

- telling people someone is gay or lesbian when that person is open about it
- being surprised (a little or a lot) when you learn that someone you admire is homosexual
- disliking someone who happens to be gay or lesbian because that person has treated you unfairly
- asking someone about their same-sex parents when you are unsure how different families are made
- saying "I've never met someone gay or lesbian before," if you didn't know you had
- respectfully asking lesbian or gay people who are out how they knew they were gay

How can you tell if the way people are with gay and lesbian people are examples of homophobia, or just people deciding which people they like or don't like? If the actions are based on the belief that homosexuality is a bad thing, then it's homophobia and it's wrong.

Homophobia 101

Homophobia might take

6

the form of...

Homophobia 101
QUIZ

Homophobia or Not?

When is what someone does or says homophobic, and when is it something else? If the person acting that way thinks that something is wrong with others just because they are gay or lesbian, that's homophobia. It's homophobia if the behaviour causes unfair treatment, harm or insult. Read the following scenarios and answer yes or no to whether it is homophobia.

Playing with Dolls

 A boy in grade one brings a doll to school and is playing at recess. Some of the other kids call him a sissy and gay.

Yes and no. Using "gay" to put someone down is always homophobic. Teasing boys who like "girl things" is actually a putdown to girls, and so is using the word "sissy" since it comes from "sister." That's not homophobia, but it is sexism.

2 Family Trees

During a discussion of families in a grade five class, Sofia complains that the information sheet the students have to fill in asks about "mom and dad." She says, "I have two moms but no dad." The teacher asks, "Were you born in a jar or something?"

MY FAMILY TREE

Yes. The form shows homophobia by not recognizing that families are different. The teacher's comment is also homophobic. That it comes from a teacher is really a problem, because students may think it's okay to say such things.

3 Health Class

You've just watched a movie in health class about puberty, body changes and growing up. When it talks about dating, it mentions only girl/boy couples.

Yes. While the video doesn't say anything specific against gay people, it talks only about straight people. It assumes everyone is straight, which isn't true.

4

Kyla is out about being a lesbian at school. Every time Kyla walks by a certain group of girls, they stop talking and stare.

Yes, if they are excluding her just because she is a lesbian. Even if they don't care she is, there is still a problem if she is being singled out.

5 Book Club, Part 1

You ask the new school librarian for some books on lesbian and gay issues for your social studies class. She looks around and can't find any, but says she will try and get some.

No. In fact, her saying she will get some is actually a good thing.

8

6 Book Club, Part 2

You ask the school librarian for some story books with same-sex families. He pulls down a box from the very top shelf with some books in it.

Yes. Why are those books way up on the top shelf while other story books are within easy reach?

7 Finding Allies

You announce to your class you want to start a Gay/Straight Alliance (GSA) at the school. A classmate asks, "Why do we need something like that here?"

No. By asking that question out of really not knowing, your classmate offers a chance to talk more about the need for a GSA.

8 Merry Christmas

They are banning Christmas songs at your school. You wonder if the song "Deck the Halls" is being banned for the line "Don we now our gay apparel..."

No. One of the original meanings of the word "gay" is "happy" or "joyful."

9 Just Dance

Kyla brings her girlfriend to the end-of-year dance. At the dance, students begin pointing and whispering.

Yes. The behaviour of the students is to target Kyla and her girlfriend and make them uncomfortable and unwelcome.

10 The Writing's on the Wall

In the boys washroom, someone has scrawled a teacher's name on the wall with the word "faggot" underneath. You want to tell someone but you are not sure if it is any more wrong than the other graffiti.

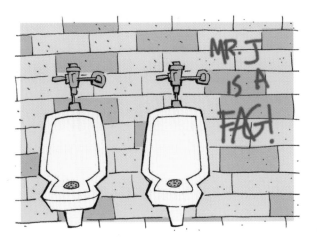

Yes and no. The graffiti is absolutely homophobic. The fact that you are unsure what to do does not make you homophobic.

Dear Conflict Counsellor

Q: The other day, one of my closest friends told me he was gay. I was seriously shocked! I mean, he doesn't look gay or act gay. He is the captain of our basketball team. I just nodded and said, "Okay." I don't know what to do.

— *Best Buddy*

A: When someone we know has the courage to share something about themselves, it is important to thank them for trusting us. Make sure your friend knows that you understand what it says about your friendship that he could tell you, even if you don't completely understand where he is coming from. It is okay to be a little freaked out or surprised, and it's okay to ask him respectful questions. It sounds like you learned something about stereotypes — ask yourself what acting gay or looking gay means. Your friend is still the same person, but now you know more about him.

Q: At school I got back a math test. I bombed it! So at my locker I blurted out, "This test was so gay!" Another student gave me dirty look and called me a homophobe. Me, a homophobe? My uncle is gay.

— *Word Watch*

A: Just because you used the word "gay" as a putdown, it doesn't mean you hate gay people. However, you did use the word in a negative way, and that seemed to equate being gay with something wrong. Be careful and watch your language.

may have never met an openly gay person, like you have. It is important to remember that we don't always think or believe the same things as our families. It is also important to remember that not all religious people think it is wrong for someone to be gay or lesbian. Finally, remember that many gays and lesbians have religious and spiritual beliefs too.

Q: I'm really confused. At home I hear my parents say really awful things about gay people. My pastor at church sometimes says them too. But one of my teachers came out and told us she is a lesbian. I think she is a really great person and, between you and me, I don't think there is anything wrong with gay people.

— *Religious Right*

A: Our families teach us lots of things about the world around us. Some families talk down gay people based on what they were taught. Some religious people also think being gay is wrong. They

Q: I'm a girl in grade eight, and for over a year, I have been having really intense feelings for a girl at my school (she's in a different classroom). I'm realizing that I might be lesbian. I'm terrified to tell my closest friends because I hear them use the word "dyke" all the time. Should I tell one of them?

— *To Be (Out) or Not to Be*

A: The decision to come out (tell someone you are gay or lesbian) is a very big decision to make. Because of prejudice and stereotypes, other people can have a homophobic reaction. It is important to think carefully about who to share this with, as it takes some people a bit of time to get used to the idea that they know someone who is gay. Think about speaking with a trusted teacher or guidance counsellor in your school. It doesn't mean you need counselling; you just want to share part of who you are.

Myths

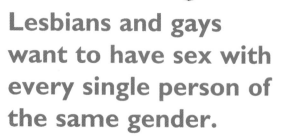

Gay men really want to be women; lesbians really want to be men.

We all have a gender identity as male or female. Being lesbian, gay or straight is about who we are attracted to, not about the gender.

Lesbians and gay men can't be parents.

Lesbians and gays want to have sex with every single person of the same gender.

This myth makes some people fearful. Remember, gays and lesbians are attracted to *some* people of the same gender, just like straight people are attracted to *some* people of the opposite gender.

It's true that two women together or two men together cannot make a child. But whether through adoption, foster parenting or help from a birth-mom or birth-dad, gays and lesbians can be parents in the way that counts — by having families.

DID YOU KNOW?

• The word "homophobia" was first used in 1972 to describe straight men who displayed a negative attitude toward homosexuals.

If you talk about lesbian and gay issues, it will make you lesbian or gay.

Talking about lesbian and gay issues doesn't change your sexual orientation. We've all studied geography right? Didn't turn anyone into a map!

All lesbians **hate** men.

Do straight women hate all other women because they are not attracted to them? Lesbians can like men as friends.

Little boys who **play with dolls** grow up to be gay.

At least three wrong ideas are in action here: Some people think (1) dolls are girl toys, so (2) boys who play with them want to be girls and (3) will be gay. Some people argue that boys who play with dolls grow up to be good dads.

All gay men talk with high voices.

Some gay men have high voices because some men with high voices are gay. Gay men can have low voices and straight men can have high voices.

• The term "Two-Spirit" is used by Aboriginal people to describe a person with both a masculine and feminine spirit.

• The 1969 Stonewall Riots in New York City are said to be the beginning of the Gay Rights Movement in North America.

The Target

You just started at a new school. In your old school, the other students liked you a lot. Many kids had been friends with you since kindergarten. This school feels different. You just joined the glee club and drama club, and a couple of boys in class start to tease and bug you, calling you "sissy," "wuss" and "gay." The other day, one of them asked you if you were really a girl, "'cause you sure act like one." Another boy heard him and shouted out, "Maybe he's into guys or something." You feel confused and angry. You've never been treated this way before.

Why are they treating you this way? It must be more than just that you're the new kid . . .

DEAR DR. SHRINK-WRAPPED...

Q: I have known I have feelings for other girls for over a year now but I haven't told anyone. My family is always saying negative things about gay people and my friends at school are always making mean jokes about "fags" and "dykes" — there's no way I'm telling any of them. On the outside I seem happy and confident, but inside I'm really depressed and confused. The other day my friends were pointing and laughing at a boy they thought was gay. I felt bad for him, but I was so terrified for myself that I joined in and called him a fag. What's wrong with me? Can I be gay *and* a homophobe?
— *Hiding Who I Am*

A: Actually, Hiding, anyone can be a homophobe, including gay and lesbian people. Sometimes lesbian and gay people who are *in the closet* (they haven't told anyone) use homophobia to deflect attention away from themselves and fit in with others. Some even date the opposite sex to hide their orientation. While only you know when it's okay for you to come out of hiding, Dr. Shrink-Wrapped can tell you that it's important for you to stop joining in the homophobia. It's obviously making you feel bad about yourself. Also, if at all possible, try to tell the kid you called names that you're sorry. No matter if he is gay or straight, he was a target of meanness and cruelty. And you can't hide from that!

Q: My girlfriend bought me a pink shirt for our anniversary, so of course I wore it to school — big mistake! From the time I walked into school, some guys gave me weird looks, pointed and laughed. Some even called me gay and a fag. My friends were pretty cool about it, but now they are being picked on too. I could stop wearing the shirt, but then my girlfriend will be really pissed. What's the big deal for a guy to wear a pink shirt!
— *Pretty Confused in Pink*

A: There's absolutely nothing wrong with guys wearing pink, Confused, except for the prejudice of others and made-up rules about gender and colour. The big deal for some is that pink is seen as a girl's colour. Therefore a guy wearing pink is acting like a girl, and guys who act like girls are gay, right? WRONG. But some people will go to absurd lengths to justify their homophobia. Maybe they are jealous of how confident you are in yourself — probably one of the qualities your girlfriend admires in you! Keep being yourself, and try to ignore the ignorant.

QUIZ

How do you handle homophobia?

Are you a **PUSHOVER**, giving in to the pressure for everyone to be — or at least appear — straight? Do you **PUSH BACK** hard against people who are homophobic? Or are you **PROUD** of who you are, gay or straight? Take this quiz and find out.

I'm a Pushover

I'm Proud

I Push Back

Your best friend at school has come out to everyone as lesbian. Now some kids are saying you're lesbian because you hang out with her so much. What do you do?

a. End your friendship.

b. Start a fight with the people who have accused you of being gay.

c. Ask your teacher if your class can host a discussion/workshop on homophobia.

a) Pushover b) Push Back c) Proud

 You do a presentation in your class on famous gay and lesbian athletes. Afterward, a classmate asks, "Why did you chose that topic, are you gay or something?" Do you . . .

a. deny loudly that you are gay?

b. tell your classmate she is stupid and walk away?

c. tell her that it makes no difference whether or not you are gay; the topic is important to challenge stereotypes?

a) Pushover b) Push Back c) Proud

 On the school bus, a group of students keep calling each other gay. When you ask them to stop, they turn on you and start loudly making homophobic remarks about you. Do you . . .

a. tell them it's really gay to call everything gay?

b. tell the bus driver and your teacher the next day?

c. just shut up and hope they leave you alone?

a) Push Back b) Proud c) Pushover

 You want to invite your school friends to your birthday party, but you are worried because they don't know you have two moms. What do you do?

a. Go ahead and invite your most-trusted friends.

b. Ask one of your moms to be away from the house that day.

c. Invite everyone and kick out anyone who asks or says anything about your moms.

a) Proud b) Pushover c) Push Back

 You came out to your class at the beginning of the school year. For a while it seemed like "no big" to others. Recently, though, a group of students began targeting you with name-calling. Do you . . .

a. call them names back?

b. announce that you were just joking when you said you were gay?

c. get your supportive friends to stand with you and tell a trusted teacher what is going on?

a) Push Back b) Pushover c) Proud

 You are sick of reading books that don't show lesbian and gay families. Do you . . .

a. go to the vice-principal and accuse the librarian of being a homophobe?

b. get a group of supportive friends together and approach the librarian about adding some books with diverse families?

c. just sit there and say nothing?

a) Push Back b) Proud c) Pushover

 A so-called friend posts on your social network wall: "Your shirt today was So Gay!" What do you do?

a. Say nothing.

b. Write something nasty back on her wall.

c. Print a copy of the homophobic posting to give your teacher; post on your social network wall: "Thanks for the compliment, but shirts don't fall in love with other shirts."

a) Pushover b) Push Back c) Proud

 For Valentine's Day, your school council asks everyone to design a card featuring a boy and a girl holding hands. As the only out gay student, you . . .

a. refuse to participate.

b. make a card showing yourself and what your boyfriend might look like if he was a girl.

c. approach the school council and explain why the contest is problematic.

a) Pushback b) Pushover c) Proud

 You see some homophobic graffiti on the bathroom walls. It started to show up shortly after your assembly speech for Pink Day. Should you . . .

a. fill the walls with nasty things about the students you think are responsible?

b. take pictures of it and show it to your parents and principal?

c. stop making speeches challenging homophobia?

a) Push Back b) Proud c) Pushover

 Your new friend at school invites you to join her at her place of worship. You like learning new things, but the speaker says really hurtful things about lesbians and gays. What do you do?

a. Go back again and say hurtful things about the speaker.

b. Thank your new friend for inviting you and don't ever mention it again.

c. Invite your new friend to your place of worship to hear a different way to talk about lesbians and gays.

a) Push Back b) Pushover c) Proud

The Target

Sick and Tired of Homophobia!

Some people still think it's okay to use mean words and stereotypes about other people. Families, followers of some religions and the media sometimes seem to give them permission to discriminate against others they think are gay or lesbian. It doesn't matter whether or not you are gay or lesbian; if homophobia is used to make you feel bad, single you out or tease, bully, and harass you, it's wrong. So, what should you do if you are the target? Here are some things to think about.

Ignore
While this is not a long-term answer or solution, sometimes it is important to try to ignore other people's ignorance by not responding to what they say.

Speak Up
If possible, challenge the name-callers. "Do you even know what gay means?" If you feel confident enough, try, "I don't care if you think I'm gay. For what it's worth, I'm not, but I don't think there is anything wrong with being gay."

Join Together
Homophobic name-calling has the same motivations as racist or sexist name-calling — fear of the unknown, feeling superior, etc. Seek out other students who care about this kind of prejudice and think about starting a student group to address all these issues schoolwide.

Get Help
Tell a teacher or a trusted adult if you experience homophobic attacks. Involve a supportive teacher or guidance counsellor in your student group. You don't have to solve this all by yourself, and adults in schools have a responsibility too.

DID YOU KNOW?

From a 2011 survey (EGALE):
- 70% of students report hearing expressions such as "that's so gay" every day in school.

dos and don'ts

✓ Do think about telling a trustworthy adult.

✓ Do use gentle humour to deflect the homophobic remarks.

✓ Do remember that being you is really important.

✓ Do keep friends in your life that care about the same things you do.

✓ Do remember that many other people are open-minded.

✓ Do remember that if you are a straight person, you are an important ally to lesbian and gay people.

✗ Don't let other people define what you like to do.

✗ Don't feel that everyone has to like you all the time.

✗ Don't blame yourself for the ignorance of others.

✗ Don't use other forms of discrimination to fight back against homophobic attitudes.

✗ Don't stop doing the things you enjoy.

Be a Know-It-All
Find out more about homophobia (and racism and sexism) and why it is a problem for everyone. Find out more about famous lesbian and gay people or famous people with lesbian and gay parents. Then you will have verbal ammunition to fire back the next time someone starts the name-calling.

Be YOU
Be confident in who you are. If you are straight, you can play an important role as an ally of lesbian and gay people. If you are figuring out that you are lesbian or gay, remember that there is nothing wrong with you — the problem is homophobia.

- Almost half (48%) reported hearing people referred to as "faggot," "lesbo" and "dyke" every day in school.

- More than a third (37%) of youth with LGBTQ parents reported being verbally harassed about the sexual orientation of their parents.

The **Homophobe**

You're not a homophobe, are **you?**

It's just that you can't tell who's gay and who's normal anymore. One kid you know just told everyone he has lesbian moms! And another told you his neighbour is gay.

"Did you just hear that?"

you say to your friends. That's gross. Those gay people had better not try anything on you!

dos and don'ts

✓ Do consider your own prejudice.

✓ Do challenge others' stereotypes.

✓ Do realize you may have already met someone who is gay or lesbian or has gay or lesbian parents.

✓ Do your best to stop using putdowns about gays and lesbians.

✓ Do examine your ideas about the gender roles we expect people to follow.

✗ Don't use the word "gay" to describe someone or something you don't like.

✗ Don't let others make you think something just because they think do.

✗ Don't assume everyone around you is straight.

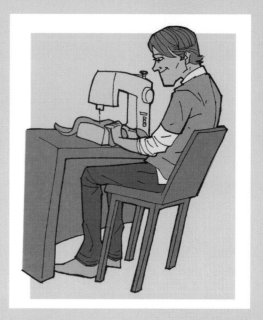

✗ Don't assume that a guy who likes things you think are "girly" is gay.

✗ Don't assume that a girl who never wears skirts and acts the way you think a boy does is a lesbian.

✗ Don't assume that everyone has the same kind of family.

The **Homophobe**

QUIZ

Are you a homophobe?

You wouldn't have a gay or lesbian friend, but that doesn't mean they *scare* you. That's what a "phobia" means, right? To be scared of something. Wrong. Homophobia is a form of prejudice towards others because of their sexual orientation. How many of the following statements are **TRUE** about you?

1. I don't want gay or lesbian people to get too close to me.

2. I believe that marriage should be between a man and a woman.

3. I think it is wrong to even use the word "gay" in school.

4. I think it is wrong to talk about lesbian and gay families with younger kids.

5. To follow my religion, I have to show gay and lesbian kids that it is wrong to be that way.

6. I believe that gay and lesbian people will be punished after they die.

7. If gay and lesbian issues are talked about in schools, it will influence kids to be gay.

8. Gay and lesbian people can choose not to be that way.

9. I'll call something "gay" to mean it is just bad or wrong.

10. If guys wear pink or act like girls, they must be gay.

11. If girls play team sports and wear their hair short, they must be lesbians.

12. They shouldn't let gay and lesbian people work with kids.

13. I have to avoid gay and lesbian people so that everyone won't think I'm that way too.

14. I have told jokes about gays and lesbians.

15. I think it's none of my business when I see people discriminating against gays and lesbians.

16 I have the right to judge other people.

17 I think it's wrong for same-sex couples to have children.

18 There's nothing I can do about homophobia.

19 I believe what my religion tells me about unnatural sex.

20 I get really uncomfortable talking to someone who I think might be gay or lesbian.

21 Gays and lesbians who are out are asking for people to treat them differently.

22 I've been called a bully.

23 I worry about someone of the same sex touching me.

24 I have been accused of homophobia.

25 I can call a gay guy a "fag" because that's what they call each other.

26 I laugh and joke when people use words like "dike" or "homonym," because it sounds like they are referring to dykes or homosexuals.

27 I think too much time and money is spent on educating people about sexual orientation.

28 I think some rights should be only for straight people.

29 I always have to laugh when someone tells a joke about gays or lesbians, so they don't think I'm one.

30 I think some school and social groups should be just for straight people.

Did you get a lot of TRUEs?

Maybe you should try to **find out more about what it means to be gay,** and talk to someone about **why you generalize** about gay people instead of **getting to know them as people.**

Your pot is boiling over!

You hear the words **"gay"** and **"lesbian"** and it makes you **totally uncomfortable.** You call things "gay" when you don't like them. Now you hear that there are students at your school with lesbian and gay parents! **What's going on?** Take a deep breath and ask yourself these questions. You might be surprised at the answers.

What Do I Know?
What exactly do you know about lesbians and gays other than what TV, your peers or your older siblings know? Are you just repeating what they say? When did you first hear the word "gay"? Was it someone using it as a putdown? In a way, you learned about homophobia before you learned what a gay person was. Be sure what you know is accurate before you repeat it.

What Am I Assuming?
Are you the kind of person who thinks all gay guys are feminine, girly and weak? Or that all lesbians are masculine and have short hair? Those are some pretty powerful stereotypes in our society. When you use "gay" as a putdown, are you assuming that everyone around is straight? How can you be sure? Is that what someone else told you? The truth is that many people you see as "normal" are different from you, or have different kinds of families. And none of them are wrong simply because they are different from what you are used to or what you think society is telling you.

When the Law Is Involved

The laws of a country can be involved in creating and maintaining homophobic attitudes — or in discouraging them. But beyond legalizing rights for gay and lesbian people, the law has to get involved when homophobic acts become criminal.

When a crime against someone is motivated by something to do with a person's identity, it can be considered a hate crime. Identity can mean a person's religion, race or sexual orientation. Someone convicted of a hate crime can be given a harsher sentence (e.g., a longer prison term) than someone convicted of a crime not involving hate.

When does a prejudiced attitude cross the line to being a hate crime? The thinking behind committing a hate crime often includes:
• a belief in the superiority of one group over another AND the idea that the superior group can use physical action to maintain their position
• the attitude that one group is somehow wrong or immoral AND the assumption that punitive action against that group is justified, or even necessary

The law can go only so far to help by giving equal rights to gay and lesbian people and cracking down on hate crimes. The best way to battle homophobia and prevent hate crimes is to tackle prejudiced attitudes with awareness and education.

Is TV the Truth?

Are you basing your understanding of lesbians and gays on a few TV shows or movies? When you see a gay or lesbian character on a show or the show is talking about gays or lesbians, ask yourself: Are they talking about lesbians and gays in a positive, realistic way or in a way that puts them down and makes fun of them for cheap laughs?

What Would I Do?

What would you do if a really good friend came out and said he or she was gay or lesbian? Remember, this is a really close friend who is showing a great deal of trust in you. Think about all the questions you might want to ask, write them down and speak with a trusted adult. Others can help you with accurate information to dispel the myths and stereotypes.

• Statistics Canada reported that in 2010, 65% of homophobic hate crimes reported to police were violent

The **Witness**

Have you seen someone **bullied, verbally or physically, for their sexual orientation?**

Have you ever heard the word "gay" used as a putdown?

Have you noticed boys getting teased for liking girly things or girls getting funny looks for being tomboys?

Did you feel like saying something at the time to stop the homophobia, but were scared or worried that the bullies might turn on you? Guess what — feeling worried about speaking up is pretty natural. Feeling worried or scared is an okay place to start, **BUT YOU CAN'T STAY THERE!**

The Power of One and the Power of Some

What can one person really do to challenge homophobia? How can you change someone's mind? Actually, **one person can make the world of difference.** It starts by recognizing that silence is a homophobe's best friend — when you say nothing, **it tells others that their words or actions are okay.**

Speaking up is not easy, and by taking a stand we risk:
- losing friends
- interfering in something we think is not our problem
- becoming the target of the same negative attention
- having people think we are gay or lesbian too
- being labelled a rat or a snitch

But by taking some risks, and not always doing it alone, **we can show others that taking a stand is possible.** That can lead to making new friends and learning new things — and it feels good too. **You can take pride in doing what you can to make things better for all of us.**

dos and don'ts

✓ Do educate yourself about homosexuality and homophobia.

✓ Do treat others with respect.

✓ Do try to stand up for someone who is being targeted.

✓ Do stand up with others trying to make change.

✓ Do get help from a trusted adult.

✗ Don't join in with the laughing or joking.

✗ Don't pretend you don't see what is going on.

✗ Don't respond with other kinds of prejudice.

✗ Don't dismiss it as no big deal.

✗ Don't stay silent because you figure it won't happen to you.

QUIZ

Do you really get it?

You are all about acceptance, and know that gay and lesbian people deserve to be treated just like everyone else. So what do you do when you witness someone being discriminated against because of homophobia? Take this quiz to see how you'd react in some high-pressure situations. This quiz has no right or wrong answers, because each situation is unique. Your answers may be different from the ones given below, but they could be right under the circumstances.

1 PINK DAY? NO WAY!

Your teacher announces that the school will hold a Pink Day event. Everyone is asked to wear something pink to take a stand against homophobia. Some students announce that they are not going to participate.

- Say that you heard that pink is now a really hot colour and lots of people — male and female — are wearing it.
- Find a picture of a sports star or other "masculine" role model wearing pink and display it in class.
- Ask the students if they are afraid that they will be targeted if they appear to support Pink Day, and who they think is homophobic.
- Find out if your teacher can make it mandatory for all kids in your class to wear pink that day.

2 DIRTY LOOKS

The new kid in class talks about her two dads and a trip they took to Niagara Falls. A group of students whisper and laugh, and give her a dirty look. What should you do?

- Support the new kid's story by carrying on the conversation and ignoring the others.
- See if the new kid wants to join your group of friends at lunch.
- Ask your teacher if there could be a class discussion on families and gay/lesbian issues.

28

3 SING A HAPPY SONG

- Ignore her text.
- Text her back: Songs can't be gay; songs can't love other songs.
- Tell her to help you list favourite and non-favourite songs, pointing out real reasons why you like them or not.
- Suggest that all your friends stop using "gay" as a putdown.
- Tell her not to text you if she is going to use prejudiced language.

5 MALL WALL

You and a friend see that someone has written something homophobic on the washroom wall. Your friend says he knows who wrote it.

- Report the graffiti to mall security.
- If one of you has a cell phone, take a picture of the offensive writing and show it to someone in the mall administration office.
- Confront the person your friend named, pointing out that putting graffiti in a public place is against the rules, and maybe the law.
- Tell the person responsible that they have to stop, or you will report them to the authorities.

4 Bully Proof

You and some friends are leaving school a little late. As you pass the schoolyard, you see a couple of students surrounding a kid. They are yelling and calling him queer and a fag.

- Stop and watch to see if things escalate to violence.
- Run back into the school and tell an adult immediately.
- Pull out your cell phone and call 911, taking a couple of pictures to show later.
- Grab your friends and head over to get the bullies to stop.

Continues . . .

The **Witness**

6 Family Diversity

Your class just had a workshop on homophobia, and talked about lesbian and gay families. After the workshop, a couple of students say they don't know why we are talking about this in school.

- Remind them that families come in all shapes and sizes.
- Point out that school is where we all learn how to better deal with the world, and that the world includes all kinds of families.
- Tell them that as long as some people have prejudices against others, there is a need to talk about homophobia and other kinds of discrimination — in and out of school.
- Tell your teacher about what you heard, and ask if the class can have a session to put the workshop in perspective.

7 TAKING A STAND ON SITTING DOWN

You're on public transit, and a family gets on. There are two dads and a son about your age. The kid is sitting separate from his dads, and some people are obviously avoiding the empty seat next to him. You hear a couple of kids start talking about how they want to throw the "baby faggot" out of the seat so they can sit down.

- Sit in the empty seat beside him.
- Tell the driver that two passengers are making threatening comments about another passenger.
- Politely tell the kid's parents what is going on. Or quietly tell the kid that maybe he should stand closer to his family.
- Offer your seat to the homophobic kids.

8 Unfriendly Action

A friend told you that a girl at her school just told her class that she is a lesbian. Your friend is freaked out — "She better not try anything on me!" She goes on to say that she posted this info on a social network.

- If she doesn't, unfriend her and alert the network administrator.
- Warn your friend that posting someone else's information on a social network can be seen as cyberbullying. Tell her she should remove it right away.
- Say you think it was brave of the girl to come out.
- Tell your friend she must be ego-tripping to think that everyone would want to hook up with her.

⑨ DO UNTO OTHERS

You invite your new friend at school to join you at your place of worship. The speaker says some hurtful things about lesbians and gays. Afterward your new friend asks why the speaker said such things. She is offended because her brother is gay and her place of worship says positive things about lesbians and gays.

- Tell her that, while it is not your place to defend the speaker or apologize for others, you don't always agree with what they say.
- Thank her for sharing with you about her family.
- Ask her about her own religion. See if you can attend her place of worship with her.
- See if you can get together a discussion group of members of your own place of worship to talk about issues.

⑩ THE THING TO DO

You are having dinner with your family when your older brother says he saw two men holding hands on the subway. "It was so disgusting!" he says. Your parents exchange looks but say nothing. You've seen this play out many times.

- Comment that you really don't see what the problem is, since the couple seemed to be minding their own business.
- Tell your brother to shut up if he can't keep his homophobic comments to himself.
- Ask your parents if they would ban prejudiced comments while you are all together.
- Excuse yourself and tell your family you'd rather eat alone than with a homophobe.

Fighting homophobia is everyone's responsibility and we need to work together. Though it might not be easy to know what to do right away, here are some more resources to help you.

Helplines

Kids Help Phone 1-800-668-6868
www.kidshelpphone.ca
LGBT Youth Line 1-800-268-9688
www.youthline.ca

Web sites

Parents and Friends of Lesbians and Gays: www.pflag.ca
EGALE Canada: www.egale.ca and www.mygsa.ca
It Gets Better campaign: http://www.itgetsbetter.org/

Books

Box Girl by Sarah Withrow. Groundwood Books, 2001.
The Boy in the Dress by David Williams. HarperCollins, 2010.
Double Play by Sara Cassidy. James Lorimer & Co., 2013.
Luv Ya Bunches by Lauren Myracle. Harry N. Abrams, 2010.
The Manny Files by Christian Burch. Aladdin, 2008.
The Popularity Papers by Amy Ignatow. Harry N. Abrams, 2010.

Other titles in the Deal With It series:

Bullying: Deal with it before push comes to shove by Elaine Slavens, illustrated by Brooke Kerrigan

Cliques: Deal with it using what you have inside by Kat Mototsune, illustrated by Ben Shannon

Cyberbullying: Deal with it and Ctrl Alt Delete it by Robyn MacEachern, illustrated by Geraldine Charette

Girlness: Deal with it body and soul by Diane Peters, illustrated by Steven Murray

Guyness: Deal with it body and soul by Steve Pitt, illustrated by Steven Murray

Image: Deal with it from the inside out by Kat Mototsune, illustrated by Ben Shannon

Teasing: Deal with it before the joke's on you by Steve Pitt, illustrated by Remie Geoffroi

Text copyright © 2013 by Steven Solomon
Illustrations copyright © James Lorimer & Company Ltd., Publishers

James Lorimer & Company Ltd., Publishers, acknowledges the support of the Ontario Arts Council. We acknowledge the financial support of the Government of Canada through the Canada Book Fund for our publishing activities. We acknowledge the support of the Canada Council for the Arts which last year invested $24.3 million in writing and publishing throughout Canada. We acknowledge the Government of Ontario through the Ontario Media Development Corporation's Ontario Book Initiative.

 Canada Council for the Arts   Conseil des Arts du Canada

 ONTARIO ARTS COUNCIL
CONSEIL DES ARTS DE L'ONTARIO

Series design: Blair Kerrigan/Glyphics

Library and Archives Canada Cataloguing in Publication

Solomon, Steven, 1966–
Homophobia : deal with it and turn prejudice into pride / by Steven Solomon ; illustrated by Nick Johnson.

(Deal with it)
Issued also in an electronic format.
ISBN 978-1-4594-0441-0 (bound).
—ISBN 978-1-4594-0442-7 (pbk.)

1. Homophobia—Juvenile literature. I. Johnson, Nick II. Title. III. Series: Deal with it (Toronto, Ont.)

HQ76.4.S65 2013 j306.76'6 C2012-908245-7

James Lorimer & Company Ltd., Publishers
317 Adelaide Street West, Suite 1002
Toronto, ON, Canada
M5V 1P9
www.lorimer.ca

Distributed in the United States by:
Orca Book Publishers
P.O. Box 468, Custer, WA
USA 98240-0468

Printed and bound in China.

Manufactured by Everbest Printing Company Ltd. in Guangzhou, China in March 2013.
Job number: 113386